My Dear SISTERS

Top cover image: *In the Garden* © Sandra B. Rast. For print information, visit www.sandra-rast-art.com or call 801.292.5686.
Bottom cover image and decorative elements in book courtesy of iStockphoto.com.

Cover and book design by Heather Ann Wiscombe, © 2008 by Covenant Communications, Inc.

Published by Covenant Communications, Inc.
American Fork, Utah

Printed in Canada
First Printing: March 2008

13 12 11 10 09 08   10 9 8 7 6 5 4 3 2 1

ISBN 13: 978-1-59811-595-6
ISBN 10: 1-59811-595-2

My Dear SISTERS

INSPIRATION FOR WOMEN FROM

GORDON B. HINCKLEY

Now, my dear sisters . . . I remind you that you are not second-class citizens in the kingdom of God. You are His divine creation. Men hold the priesthood. Yours is a different role, but also extremely important. Without you, our Father's plan of happiness would be frustrated and have no real meaning. You are fifty percent of the membership of the Church and mothers of the other fifty percent. No one can dismiss you lightly.

There has come to you as your birthright something beautiful and sacred and divine. Never forget that. Your Eternal Father is the great Master of the universe. He rules over all, but He also will listen to your prayers as His daughter and hear you as you speak with Him. He will answer your prayers. He will not leave you alone.

As you create a home, don't get distracted with a lot of things that have no meaning for you or your family. Don't dwell on your failures, but think about your successes. Have joy in your home. Have joy in your children. Have joy in your husband. Be grateful for the journey.

~ Marjorie Pay Hinckley

You are young enough that the future world of which you dream still lies ahead of you. Each is a child of God. Each of you is a creature of Divinity. You are literally a daughter of the Almighty. There is no limit to your potential. If you will take control of your lives, the future is filled with opportunity and gladness. You cannot afford to waste your talents or your time. Great opportunities lie ahead of you.

First, educate your hands
and your minds. You
belong to a church which
espouses education. . . . Get
all the education you can.
Train yourselves to make a
contribution to the society in
which you will live. There is
an essence of the divine in the
improvement of the mind.

My dear sisters, you marvelous women who have chosen the better part, I stand in great admiration for all that you do. I see your hands in everything. . . . Many of you are mothers, and that is enough to occupy one's full time. You are companions—the very best friends your husbands have or ever will have. . . . You are nurses. With every illness that comes along, you are the first to be told about it and the first to respond with help. In cases of serious sickness, you are at the bedside day and night, comforting, encouraging, ministering, praying.

Some few of the greatest characters of scripture have been women of integrity, accomplishment, and faith. We have Esther, Naomi, and Ruth of the Old Testament. We have Sariah of the Book of Mormon. We have Mary, the very mother of the Redeemer of the world. . . . Crossing through His life we have Mary and Martha, and Mary of Magdala. She it was who came to the tomb that first Easter morning. And to her, a woman, He first appeared as the resurrected Lord.

of home is not dependent on wealth, ss, or beauty, or luxury. Everything depends on the mother.

The women in our lives are creatures

endowed with particular qualities, divine

qualities, which cause them to reach out

in kindness and with love to those about

them. We can encourage that outreach

if we will give them opportunity to give

expression to the talents and impulses that

lie within them. In our old age my beloved

companion said to me quietly one evening,

"You have always given me wings to fly,

and I have loved you for it."

A group of ancient Roman women were, with vanity, showing their jewels one to another. Among them was Cornelia, the mother of two boys. One of the women said to her, "And where are your jewels?" to which Cornelia responded, pointing to her sons, "These are my jewels." Under her tutelage, and walking after the virtues of her life, they grew to become . . . two of the most persuasive and effective reformers in Roman history. For as long as they are remembered and spoken of . . . their mother will be remembered and spoken of with praise also.

A house is no home unless it contains food and fire for the mind as well as for the body... -Margaret Fuller, woman in the 19th century

I would wish that all of you women . . . would not have to go out into the marketplace to labor for income. But I know that for some of you this may be a necessity, and you will be better equipped to do so if your hands and minds are trained. Furthermore, whether it is applied to earning a living or not, education is an investment that never ceases to pay dividends of one kind or another.

Have you ever contemplated the wonders of yourself, the eyes with which you see, the ears with which you hear, the voice with which you speak? No camera ever built can compare with the human eye. No method of communication ever devised can compare with the voice and the ear. No pump ever built will run as long or as efficiently as the human heart. No computer or other creation of science can equal the human brain. What a remarkable thing you are. You can think by day and dream by night.

You must know . . . that

you are not alone in this

world. There are hundreds

of thousands of you. You live

in many lands. You speak

various languages. And every

one of you has something

divine within you. You are

second to none. You are

daughters of God.

'You are the caretaker of the generati
giver,' the Sun told the woman. 'You
this universe.' — Sioux Sun Creation

There is no such thing as
the perfect mother. . . . We
just do the best we can with
the help of the Lord, and
who knows, these children
who are struggling to be free
may someday rise up and call
us blessed.

~ Marjorie Pay Hinckley

The whole gamut of human endeavor is now open to women. There is not anything that you cannot do if you will set your mind to it. I am grateful that women today are afforded the same opportunity to study for science, for the professions, and for every other facet of human knowledge. You are as entitled as are men to the Spirit of Christ, which enlightens every man and woman who comes into the world.

knowledg

You are creatures of divinity; you are daughters of the Almighty. Limitless is your potential. Magnificent is your future.

It is the natural instinct of women to reach out in love to those in distress and need.

How much more beautiful would be the world and the society in which we live if . . . every mother regarded her children as the jewels of her life, as gifts from the God of heaven, who is their Eternal Father, and brought them up with true affection in the wisdom and admonition of the Lord.

You are the keepers of the homes. You give encouragement to your husbands. You teach and nurture your children in faith. For some of you life is difficult and even bitter. But you complain so very little and do so very much. How deeply indebted we are to you!

The future destiny of the child is always the work of the m
— Napoleon Bonaparte

What a remarkable thing it is to witness the love of good women one for another. They mingle together in the bonds of love with friendship and respect for each other.

E. T. Sullivan once wrote these interesting words: "When God wants a great work done in the world or a great wrong righted, he goes about it in a very unusual way. He doesn't stir up his earthquakes or send forth his thunderbolts. Instead, he has a helpless baby born, perhaps in a simple home and of some obscure mother. And then God puts the idea into the mother's heart, and she puts it into the baby's mind. And then God waits."

And even though you marry, education will be of great benefit to you. Don't just drift along, letting the days come and go without improvement in your lives. The Lord will bless you as you make the effort. Your lives will be enriched and your outlook broadened as your minds are opened to new vistas and knowledge.

Woman is God's supreme creation. Only after the earth had been formed, after the day had been separated from the night, after the waters had been divided from the land, after vegetation and animal life had been created, and after man had been placed on the earth, was woman created; and only then was the work pronounced complete and good.

I wish to reemphasize my deep gratitude,

my profound appreciation for the women of

this Church and the tremendous sons and

daughters you are teaching, training, helping

to take their places in the world. But the

task will never be finished. It will never be

complete. May the light of the Lord shine

upon you. May the Lord bless you in your

great and sacred work.

Develop some intellectual curiosity. If you have it, you will never be bored. If you haven't, cultivate it, hold fast to it. Never let it go. To the intellectually curious, the world will always be full of magic, full of wonder. You will be interesting to your friends, to your spouse, and a joy to your children. You will be alive to all of the wonderful possibilities of this world.

~ Marjorie Pay Hinckley

It is and has been your opportunity to mingle together as sisters who love and honor and respect one another, to bring the blessings of pleasant sociality into the lives of tens of thousands who, without you, would be left in very bleak and lonely circumstances.

It is for us, sisters, to make certain that underlying everything we do in the course of a day is a settled faith in God, in His existence, personality and attributes. There must be faith in the restored gospel and in its power to save; faith in the divine mission of the Savior. This faith will give us the power to work righteousness. God bless us all to do what needs to be done by our hands, and to do it cheerfully and with joy.

~ Marjorie Pay Hinckley

It is so important that you . . . women get

all of the education that you can . . . even

by study and by faith. Education is the key

which will unlock the door of opportunity

for you. It is worth sacrificing for. . . . You

will be able to make a great contribution

to the society of which you are a part, and

you will be able to reflect honorably on the

Church of which you are a member.

If anyone can change

the dismal situation into

which we are sliding, it is

you. Rise up, O women

of Zion, rise to the great

challenge which faces you.

From the beginning it has been your most
important responsibility to see that no one
goes hungry, to see that no one goes without
adequate clothing, that no one goes without
shelter. It has been and is your responsibility
to visit your sisters wherever they may
be found . . . to assure them of love and
concern and interest. It is and has been
your opportunity to tear away the curtain
of darkness that enshrouds those who are
illiterate and to bring into their lives the
light of understanding as you teach them to
read and to write.

What a wonderful thing you have done as mothers. You have given birth and nurtured children. You have entered into a partnership with our Father in Heaven to give mortal experience to His sons and daughters. They are His children and they are your children, flesh of your flesh, for whom He will hold you responsible. You have rejoiced over them, and in many cases you have sorrowed. They have brought you happiness as no one else could. They have brought you pain as none other could.

And to you women . . . .
You too can take on the luster
of Christ. You too can be
strong and encouraging and
beautiful and helpful . . . .
We can stand for truth and
goodness, and we will not
stand alone. Moreover, we
shall have the unseen forces
of heaven to assist us.

You have the potential to become anything to which you set your mind. You have a mind and a body and a spirit. With these three working together, you can walk the high road that leads to achievement and happiness. But this will require effort and sacrifice and faith.

My heart reaches out to you. I appreciate you. I honor you. I respect you. What a tremendous force for good you are. You are the strength of the present, the hope of the future. You are the sum of all the generations that have gone before, the promise of all that will come hereafter.

hope of the future

You are daughters of God.
You are members of The
Church of Jesus Christ of
Latter-day Saints. In your
youth you speak of the future,
and it is bright with promise.
You speak of hope and faith
and achievement. You speak of
goodness and love and peace.
You speak of a better world
than we have ever known.

God bless you, dear friends.
Do not trade your birthright
as a mother for some bauble
of passing value. Let your
first interest be in your home.
The baby you hold in your
arms will grow quickly as the
sunrise and the sunset of the
rushing days.

In this work there must be commitment. There must be devotion. We are engaged in a great eternal struggle that concerns the very souls of the sons and daughters of God. We are not losing. We are winning. We will continue to win if we will be faithful and true. We can do it. We must do it. We will do it. There is nothing the Lord has asked of us that in faith we cannot accomplish.

You provide inspiration. You provide balance. You constitute a vast reservoir of faith and good works. You are an anchor of devotion and loyalty and accomplishment. No one can gainsay the great part you play in the onward rolling of this work across the earth.

Never forget that you came to earth as a child of the divine Father, with something of divinity in your very makeup. The Lord did not send you here to fail. He did not give you life to waste it. He bestowed upon you the gift of mortality that you might gain experience—positive, wonderful, purposeful experience—that will lead to life eternal . . . May God bless you richly and abundantly, my dear . . . friends, His wonderful daughters.

iv-1
Seeking Shiloah © Joseph Brickey. For more information, visit www.olivewoodbooks.com or call 801.373.2787.

2-3
The Annunciation © James Christensen. Courtesy of Greenwich Workshop. For print information, visit www.greenwichworkshop.com or call 800.243.4246.

4–5
Closely Knit © Julie Rogers. For more information go to www.julierogersart.com or call 435.648.2607.

6–7
Song of Praise © Greg Olsen Publishing Inc. For more information, visit www.gregolsenart.com or call 208.888.2585.

8–9
A Family Home Evening © Bruce Clovis Smith.

10–11
Gardening Scene from *Daughter of a King* Series © David Lindsley. For print information, visit www.davidlindsley.com

12–13
Why Weepest Thou © Simon Dewey. Courtesy of Altus Fine Arts. For print information, visit www.altusfinearts.com or call 801.763.9788.

14–15
Companions © Robert Duncan. For more information, visit www.robertduncanstudios.com or call 435.657.0500.

16–17
Seed of Faith © Jay Bryant Ward. Courtesy of Altus Fine Arts. For print information, visit www.altusfinearts.com or call 801.763.9788.

18–19
Sabboth Study © Sheri Lynn Boyer Doty. For more information, visit www.sheridoty.com or call 801.949.5657.

20–21
Under a Clear Blue Sky © Mike Malm. For more information, visit www.mikemalm.com.

22–23
Shoshone Princess © Carol Harding. For more information, call 801.785.2446.

24–25
Heather © William Whitaker. For print information, visit www.williamwhitaker.com.

26–27
Memory (Hilltop Farm) © Sheri Lynn Boyer Doty. For more information, visit www.sheridoty.com or call 801.949.5657.

28–29
She Turned to Him © Del Parson.

30–31
Refuge © Liz Lemon Swindle. Courtesy of Foundation Arts. For print information, visit www.foundationarts.com.

32–33
Remember My Son © Anne Marie Oborn. For more information, visit www.anneoborn.com or call 801.298.5694.

34–35
Teach Me to Walk in the Light © Emily Dyches. Courtesy of Altus Fine Arts. For print information, visit www.altusfinearts.com or call 801.763.9788.

36–37
Wash Day © Lynde Mott. Courtesy of Altus Fine Arts. For print information, visit www.altusfinearts.com or call 801.763.9788.

38–39
Evening Among the Roses © Trent Gudmundsen. For more information, visit www.trentgudmundsen.com.

40–41
Sitting on a Thonet Bentwood, 1979 © Kent Goodliffe. Courtesy of Springville Museum of Art.

42–43
Delicate Rose © Michael Albrechtsen. For more information, visit www.michaelalbrechtsen.com or call 913.780.9694.

44–45
Children of Light © Anne Marie Oborn. For more information, visit www.anneoborn.com or call 801.298.5694.

46–47
Chore Time © Valoy Eaton. For more information visit www.valoyeaton.com.

48–49
Quilting Bee © Lynde Mott. Courtesy of Altus Fine Arts. For print information, visit www.altusfinearts.com or call 801.763.9788.

50–51
Roses of Santa Fe © William Whitaker. For print information, visit www.williamwhitaker.com.

52–53
Priceless Treasures © Sandra B. Rast. For print information, visit www.sandra-rast-art.com or call 801.292.5686.

54–55
Add to Your Faith Virtue © Walter Rane. For more information, visit www.thestable.com.

56–57
The Pioneer © Robert Barrett. For more information, visit www.robertbarrett.com or call 801.374.0940.

58–59
Rose Garden Moment © Anne Marie Oborn. For more information visit www.anneoborn.com or call 801.298.5694.

60–61
The Pink Ribbon © James Christensen. Courtesy of Greenwich Workshop. For print information, visit www.greenwichworkshop.com or call 800.243.4246.

62–63
Harvest © J. Kirk Richards. For more information, visit www.jkirkrichards.com.

64–65
Hand in Hand © Greg Olsen Publishing Inc. For more information, visit www.gregolsenart.com or call 208.888.2585.

66–67
Sisters © Anne Marie Oborn. For more information, visit www.anneoborn.com or call 801.298.5694.

68–69
A Mother's Love © Dixon Leavitt. For more information visit www.dixonleavitt.com.

70–71
In the Garden © Sandra B. Rast. For print information, visit www.sandra-rast-art.com or call 801.292.5686.

72–73
In the Hands of the Potter © Julie Rogers. For more information, visit www.julierogersart.com or call 435.648.2607.

74–75
Peace © Trent Gudmundsen. For more information, visit www.trentgudmundsen.com.